THE UNLIT PATH BEHIND THE HOUSE

THE HUGH MACLENNAN POETRY SERIES

Editors: Allan Hepburn and Carolyn Smart

TITLES IN THE SERIES

The Unlit Path
Behind the House

Margo Wheaton

McGill-Queen's University Press

Montreal & Kingston • London • Chicago

© Margo Wheaton 2016

ISBN 978-0-7735-4677-6 (paper)
ISBN 978-0-7735-9889-8 (ePDF)
ISBN 978-0-7735-9890-4 (ePUB)

Legal deposit first quarter 2016
Bibliothèque nationale du Québec

Printed in Canada on acid-free paper that is 100% ancient forest
free (100% post-consumer recycled), processed chlorine free

McGill-Queen's University Press acknowledges the support of the
Canada Council for the Arts for our publishing program. We also
acknowledge the financial support of the Government of Canada
through the Canada Book Fund for our publishing activities.

Library and Archives Canada Cataloguing in Publication

Wheaton, Margo, author
   The unlit path behind the house / Margo Wheaton.

Poems.
Includes bibliographical references.
Issued in print and electronic formats.
ISBN 978-0-7735-4677-6 (paperback). –
ISBN 978-0-7735-9889-8 (pdf). –
ISBN 978-0-7735-9890-4 (ePUB)

I. Title.

PS8595.H3675U56 2016   C811'.6   C2015-908292-7
                                       C2015-908293-5

This book was typeset by Interscript in 9.5/13 New Baskerville.

CONTENTS

IV

This is our misfortune
and maybe
our small grace:

we throw words at the dark
and the dark comes
back to us ...

– John Thompson

SEEING ME HOME

What did the neighbours think?

Drifting by their windows,
going to check on the youngest,
maybe help with homework

or looking up during commercials
and gazing outside, the sitcom
still fresh

or nudging each other, eyebrows
up to the bottom of the blinds, motioning
Tell Mom, she's *gotta* come see this:

the boy with the bad reputation carrying
a girl unconscious in his arms.

Steady as a procession, he passes
beneath the eyes of the houses, blind
to the blue flicker of screens,
occupied with the task at hand

her mouth open and oblivious
as an accident victim's,
bra strap showing, a sandal gone.

He carries her the way someone carries
a child to bed, breath-held careful
so as not to disturb any dreams,
incur cries.

Seen like this,
through the window of a poem,
they could be a metaphor.

Could be Lear carrying Cordelia,
her body all our unanswered questions

or a man lifting a bride
over the threshold into the white room
of a new life

or Abraham bearing Isaac,
grim and beaten
but believing.

Believe me
they are none of these things.

This is just that goddamned Melanson kid
managed to get the whole neighbourhood high
lugging that Wheaton girl back to her father's place
been drunk since her mother left,
girl's not gonna make nineteen.

This is just the pain
in living, impossible to bear
and bodies, bearing it.

I

FIREFLIES

Tonight, they are low green
notes in the field, a barely
audible humming

reminding you
of all that you know

about inwardness.

You came out here
to rescue patio chairs from an
oncoming storm,

get a read on the sky before
heading to town.

             Now, you're leaning
against the balcony rail, tuned
to the roaming cadence
of their coming

and going,

breathing slower,
your body a page

upon which the singing
world writes.

MISPLACED

For weeks, morning's arrived
at your door like an unwelcome guest
with so much to tell you.

All day, you carry the gift it brings,
handed in by the clamouring light
that infuses your white cotton curtains,

then, given by dew beading
alyssum: the feeling

that you've misplaced
something. Laid it down

such a long time ago, you cannot
imagine where to start looking.

Late in the afternoon, when the day's
beginning to close its eyes, tired
of trying to light your way,

you notice the look of expectation

forming on your daughter's face
as she tries to coax a caterpillar
to come out from its house of shade,

and you know
when you find what's been missing,
you'll share it like cake,

break it like bread
and be filled.

WHAT BEGINS WITH ENDINGS

for M.S.

The day, for example, remembered
with startling clarity.

How the light rose over
the salmon-spotted rocks, threw
the pink dots into relief.

Tonight you can see it:
the light's love, its gentle attention –
an old painter with a magnificent eye.
                    In the arid landscape

of your divorce, a few portraits
wildly scrounged from the attic:

her face those times
you surprised her with orchids –
remembered to ask. How gratitude

shines like a missing earring
discovered in a boot-toe,

and the kitchen always filled
with steam, the steady complaint
of the kettle's mouth.

All the angry words and overturned
glasses as you tried to escape Sorrow's
frayed noose of weeping. The world

a green canvas outside the door.

Now this, unexpected at four
in the morning: the baffled ends

of emptiness drawing breath
on the pillow beside you.

          The next day, her scarves
don't seem so offensive; and she
doesn't flinch at your ties, or the anxious way
you keep clearing your throat.

          You could tell her
this time about the way her eyes
still hold you in their open net ·

like arms outstretched
on unmarked water, tell her

you understand everything now.

WAITING

is a sacrament.

There's no way to know
if the one you yearn for,

want to taste like salt
bestowed by a sudden wind

will arrive this time,

that his feet will carve a path
to your door, the tiered night
unfolding like water.

Outside, the porch light
is keeping its vigil, more constant
than the human heart

that can only try
and fail to be faithful,

to be more than its
animal beating.

Still, somehow, you've become
love's attendant,

sit motionless at the kitchen table,
refusing to distract yourself
from the silence

so fully

are you trying
to perfect this prayer.

INSTRUCTION

Outside the painted windows
of the schoolhouse room where we're talking
about inspiration,

the wind's rifling through the trees
like it's searching through a kitchen drawer.

This gunmetal day's reminding us
of the way things are, vulnerability
pressed against our bones. Still, that delirious

smell through the door of the not-yet-
why-not-try of summer air
in a few moments of voltage

right before rain

and the stale,
two o'clock taste of self
like old gum in the mouth is forgotten
in a rush of water sounding through leaves –

the homemade sign
in the gravel lot out back pointing to *More
Parking and Entrances* is suddenly singing,

bluer somehow,
the weather-skinned letters a line of Blake's angels
announcing

take this path
the moments make: a portal,

a way in.

PAUSE

At the edge of these murmuring
woods are words you know
and cannot say –

the ones your body's refused
to stop speaking.

You're certain that within
this dark population of resolute pines
and maniacal roots,

in the damp austerity
that's been made by days
of exhalations,

is a name for the loneliness
wrapped inside the torn cloth
of the train whistle's cry,

for the way shadows thicken
under the lilac.

Words to formulate the question
fading light is the answer to.

What's keeping you, then,
from entering this place?

Has you staring instead at needles,
each one indistinguishable
and alone,

at the way each piece
of frozen rain dissolves
the moment

it touches the ground.

Deep in the room your heart
has been carving,

you know the sound
of that erasure.

GIFTS

I

Full moon, silent as bone. A hole
cut out of the twittering sky.

There is no geography: street signs in sand.
Forget how to read.

Your skull an egg, at home in my palm;
snap my wrist, it'd crack you clean.

Vowels scattered all over the floor.
Poems are white flags.

Wind. Waves. Immeasurable sea –
gifts we can't open; we don't have hands.

II

Night drops you like a hook into my kitchen
the world still on you, slick as oil.

Sun hits kettle, toaster, faucet –
suddenly everything's possible.

A homeless man in the park, talking to geese.
The years unfurl from his face like film.

My father's feet walking the garden,
their soundless love of the land.

Lift your arms behind your head: elbows point
to the sky.

UNSUMMONED

for W.

This afternoon's an outstretched hand, sky
a pale, unmarked page. September
lets itself in through the window,

audacious as freshly sharpened pencils,
tossing us a ribbon of birdsong written
on a sheet long as memory.

There's no denying its genius,
the beauty in those unschooled notes,
but you surprise me by reaching over
and banging the window shut.

It's too loud. Distracting.

The sound's interrupting an inner
refrain, that fierce orchestration
of meaningless tasks you perform.
                    Obsession:
an adored conductor you'd give up
the skin of your fingers
to please.

Days like this undo you, effortlessly.
Achieve a startling note of blue
and carry it without wavering

while sickness broods,
tallies your failings.

                    Helpless,
I bring you the books
you've asked for,

pray some image
or line will send desire reaching inside
like the light that's spilling
across your hand,

nervously drumming
the kitchen table

as birds exhale
song.

SIGHTING

I'm so startled I stop, mid-stride, arms forgotten in flight,
grocery bag headlong into my thigh. There, in the oak
beside the rectory, sewn into its highest branches –
camouflaged, precious, the brain alive ticking inside its
thorny crown – a crow up to her knees, building her kitchen
of grasses and hair.

Of course: crow mom. I forgot, caught up in their public
persona. Zipped in black leather, each one's quintessential, a
convincing James Dean. Their cries too craggy, too raw to be
romance – they're soliloquies, arguments with the Director.
Been compulsively cast as outlaws who won't band, wed to
the sky.

I must have thought they multiplied in a warehouse some-
where like a Warhol print, indifferent as soup cans.

This morning, the nest looked empty, abandoned … but no.
Stationed on top of an unsuspecting cross growing out of its
steeple, a disobedient weather vane stuck in one direction,
nailed to home: crow, watching. Patrolling her kingdom. A
shout against the subordinate sky, body tensed into just one
word, bold type, all capital letters.

Don't.

Keep your hands away from that tree. My garden of secrets.

FOR PAUL, AWAY

For six weeks in spring,
the phone line bears the mammalian
weight of the things we can't say.

We circle it carefully, speak
in ellipses.

*

You tell me you lit
a candle for Donna this afternoon
in Rome's oldest church. The steady,

solemn flame of her illness.

*

Yesterday, I caught you
in a lie –

you swore you touched
the famous foot of St Peter's statue
in the basilica as I'd asked you to
for luck; then, when pressed,

confessed you forgot.

      In the silence,

the marble
of sudden estrangement.

*

During supper on the piazza, you put
down your fork, started to worry
about our daughter.

      It was two-thirty here.

In the public gardens, the beating
wings of a dozen pigeons
encased her laughter,

like brackets,
enfolded her.

*

Four days, four nights
until you're back. The morning
of your return like the first glimpse
of a city's lights.

From opposite ends, we walk
towards it.

NORTH STREET

This time of year, the days end
sudden as someone slamming
a cellar door.

In the late afternoon, cars go by
flashlighting leaves that step
from closets
of shadows, slick
and outspoken as new vinyl shoes.

Like a soon-to-be-discovered
star transfixing a crowded tavern before
the end of the second song,

in October, the trees don't have
to raise their voices to get
your attention.

One's calling you now
from the parking lot beside
the school, branches creaking,

sequined with rain and though
you've seen red maples
in autumn,

like a heart

its breaking is the first
in the world.

BACK

When the door flew open, I saw
at once you couldn't be saved:

the booze had moved in. Your eyes
flat stones to be thrown against faces.

Not a goddamn dime and a house filled
with empties. *Hold me. Help me.*
I hate you.

Your broken voice like a talking doll's
whose string has been pulled once
too often.

How I wanted to make you better.

Take you to some childhood room,
lay you sweetly on the bed
and close your eyes with my nine-year-
old thumbs.

There's no place to hide you.

At dawn, the babies in your blood
will start to wail like minutes-young
birds.

You want the box-springs
of the nest. Dirt's cool sheet.
Are scratching your way back

to the earth, each pull on the bottle
a sure migration. A rowing home.

WORK

Minutes before the thunderstorm,
my neighbour goes into her garden
to rescue the peonies.

Their pink and white billowy
heads are weighted with the worries
of saints,

tremulous visions of wind
and destruction.

Soon she'll leave for her job
at the library, gather boxes to take
to the prison.

As the afternoon light is turning front lawns
into gilded pages, my neighbour
walks the length of cinder block halls,

her freckled arms laden
with books.

For three hours each week,
she studies the cryptic narration
of lines scrawled at the corners of eyes
and mouths,

tries to read what's
written there.

                      At suppertime,
she'll return to the quiet
house of her husband's gaze,

place fruit and rolls
on a wooden table,

and watch the sun through the kitchen window
bowing its bloody head to the ground,
the men's sealed faces

floating through her thoughts like music
from another room,

a refrain that ties her
to the world.

II

TORN

for Rhonda Bourgeois 1964–1992

I

      Then, in the dark room,
I opened my eyes, torn from a thick
batting of sleep without knowing why,
a rider thrown

clear of an ambling dream.

In the empty field of that hour, only
the sound of my father's snores
rolling back and forth across
the hall, dark

and satisfied.

It didn't let go, the feeling –
as though being broadcast through
air – that something was wrong

like when you suddenly wonder, miles
from home, if you'd turned off
the stove, if the door had really

locked behind you.

I went downstairs, met
the unconscious hum of the house:

phlegmy mantra of the ancient fridge,
the static croon of stereo speakers
left on by mistake. From the porch,

the soft ruckus of summer air
trying to jimmy a patio door.

I checked every room, eventually
climbed the stairs resigned. Went numb
when I learned they'd estimated

his car had drifted into your lane,
sent you into the black-orange
of the collision

at four a.m.

the roar in your ears
as I was sitting at the kitchen table,
listening to the night's long turn

as if there was nothing
in the world but time.

II

We sat there in your mother's kitchen
the day after it happened,
just feeling it –

the slow drag of death

bowing the heads of your sisters.
All five arranged around the table
as if at a séance,

staring ferociously
into its centre.

(The youngest in blue,
eight months pregnant
and inward, all that new life.)

Now and then,
we glanced up,

looked blankly at the others,
tossed bits of conversation into
the air like decoys.

Your mother gave us
one good story:

She'd stayed out all night and this
would've been the third time in a row
or some foolish thing. Out running the roads

with that Jeffrey Melanson. Came waltzing in
at six in the morning lit up like a Christmas tree,
singing John Prine, smelling like a brewery

and I said, "That's it. You're grounded."
She looked at me big-eyed as Bambi and said,
"Does that mean I can't go to the concert tonight?"

She slept most of that day then made up excuses
to enter whatever room I was in, go walking by me
real slow turning up her nose. I said, "You can act

like Lady Di all you like, my dear, but you're doing
it inside the house." Later, there was this lump
on her bed. (We all started to smile, knowing full well.)

Blankets done up like she was still there. Of course,
she picked the exact minute I ran upstairs to slip in
through the window, get under the covers.

She sat up when I walked back in. Rubbed
her eyes and looked around confused, waking up
in the middle of the night and all, then said

in this pissed-off little voice, serious
as you please, "What are you doing up this late?
You should be in bed."

We sputtered with laughter then,
able to breathe. Straightened our backs
and gazed out the window, grinning,

before the bulky silence
of your absence bowed
our heads back to the floor

firmly as a hairdresser's hands

and left us there,
chastised. Stuck.

III

Something funny
your mother insisted
instructing me on the eulogy,

your mother white with grief,
bone-white from the weight of it,
the living room a goddamn flower shop.

Just make sure you put something
funny in there.

Not much I could lift
from the way I found out,
on the phone with that RCMP officer:

It's got to be one of the worst I've seen
and I've been looking at these things
for close to twenty years now. Both cars

just a ball of flames by the time I got there.
The guy's front end sitting right up
in her driver's seat. We're trying

to identify the passengers. Her sister
thought one of them might have been you.

Whatever sound I made
must have startled him then
because he stopped,

allowed a brief silence
and said

*In these things, it's the impact
that kills. I'm telling you*

she died just like that.

IV

Your eight-year-old daughter
left motherless.

She stands there
looking puzzled after they
tell her,

cocks her head to one
side and says, astonished
at adult stupidity,

no.

That *couldn't* happen
to Mommy.

Instinctively feeling
for narrative.

Squinting up, her face
seems to say let me
speak to the artist

in charge.

V

By the time evening
came, how the silence
had changed –

a low Gregorian note
reaching through it,

inviolable

as the sick sense of timing
that tore you from your knowledge
of night, sudden glass, the blood's

journeying up and out.

You were driving across
the Cobequid hills on your way
back from Halifax, harbour city,

a symbol that fit you entirely,
friend, finally daring happiness
like a stowaway.

The tenacity that steered you through
a childhood famous on our street
for its messy Dickensian plot

had served you like a guiding star
as you rowed against the expected
trajectory of your life.

Just weeks before, the social work degree
you'd earned in spite of your eighth-grade
education. The glowing allure of a desk,
decent paycheque, the self-respect

of having eluded ghosts,
the ones that stalked you down the stairs even
after he was cast behind bars. *Dealt with.*

Telling me at the kitchen table
in my childhood home –

four doors and the length
of the ball field from yours –

how you'd found it, the gold within,
and me knowing the waves the rats the heat
you'd braved to get there. Rhonda,

you were lovely as sails

the last time I saw you. Casually
waving across one shoulder, backing
onto the street and then pulling away.

> Days later, Karen told me
> your graduation ring was the only
> thing they'd recovered.
>
> How it must have looked
> in the day's first light,
> inside all that wreckage, whole
>
> and shining.

III

BROKEN

This afternoon, the sky's stretching grey
and unconcerned – who knows
when its reign will be broken?

                    In the woods again,
you're trying to imagine the weight of snow
on the backs of willow branches
that cannot refuse to bear it

and bow, aching to know how to carry
your own suffering so well.

You've come here with all your dilemmas,
a history of ruined love inscribed along the length
of your shoulders, written into your neck
and arms, failure

the only gift you've brought
for the reticent gods, recalling the startling
wholeness of berries,

the balsam needle's abiding green.

                    Now, faced with the refrain
of the forest breathing, you can't
think of a single sentence to formulate
an invocation:

nothing here knows you're broken.

Both halves of the wind-
snapped twig perfectly encased
in ice. Crystals

lining the jagged teeth
of the storm-felled pine.

Studying them,
you suddenly want to go even further
into these woods,

       lose yourself
in the language
of stillness, words it will take

your whole lifetime
to hear.

LINES TOWARDS PRAISING THE START
OF NOVEMBER

I

The earth's talking out
loud to itself,

running through pencilled items
on a checklist titled *The Cycle
of Things,*

a conversation
our bodies decipher.

*

All week, a primal tang's left
hanging in the air:

what October knew.

In the mornings, a cold,
second taste:

tart dryness
of a coming still.

*

Light pouring in white-
gold bars against plastic treat bags
snarled in asters,

its steady,
philanthropic gaze

lavished on the baffled
world.

*

On the weekend, before the park
closed for the season,

we walked through woods

on paths that carried us back to the highway
before the afternoon's glimmering
fragments were taken

like jacks
by the day's closing hand.

*

See for yourself. The sky's already
bartered mauves and pinks

for violet

and the cello that leans
against the walls of the afternoon
has unfastened its voice: lines

in dusk's apologia.

II

Early this morning, you left again
to walk the leaf-choked field
past the railroad tracks

because you keep mistaking hearts
for compasses, confusing
embraces with fire and water;

because your life's become
a bundle you've been carrying on your back
and now you can't
seem to remember
when it first was hefted there.

Who filled it
with such heavy stones.

*

There's no moon tonight.
The field is empty.

On the horizon, an orange wolfish
clatter of lights from the mall:

a dollar store brooch
someone's pinned to the dark.

*

This sharp air's
orchestral with the advent of rain,

mist absently
soaking your jacket.

The poverty
of expectation, desire
emptying every moment

and standing before you

the elliptical field –
ground so speechless, so
uneven, you briefly imagine a long row of candles
across the stone bed of its body:

a path to the opposite side
where you're certain by now
a garden must be. Quiet,

a home.

III

By the amber ring
of a guttering candle,

in a bed in a dark
room filling with draft,

you twist towards me.

Drink light
from my skin.

From my desk, I can see sidewalks
strewn with the sun's tempera. Light

impervious to its surroundings: a college student
who's ended up at the wrong party and hasn't

been propositioned yet. Gleefully
toasting everyone.

*

Morning continues. A wide-eyed actor
who hasn't learned to improvise. We long

to forget the lines we know.

*

Partly scribbled sheets at my elbow:
cold company. Words

are strangers at a party
we spy on through windows. Swapping

office gossip, their outrageous lies.

*

      Maybe something will happen –
a sudden knock, unexpected call. The city

breaking down my door, impatient with
iambics. Maybe.

*

Twilight will come like a promise
or threat, determined to rouse

the old instincts. We'll stare
at the ceiling. The hills

steaming outside.

*

Something cooing: pigeons tucked
inside the roof folds. That much
the ear

can identify – the source
of sound. But never

the reason for all this singing.

how the inner world turns
into landscape: a kingdom,

a desert, the pathway
through woods.

You don't have to tell me
I figure there, that you're stationed
in me. It's the reason we crane

apart when we're seated together,
each waiting for the moment
the other will leave

so that we can begin.

*

Walking across the lobby to get
to the reading, you briefly

place your hand on my back, steer me
through the right door.

Later, memory's endless spool:
your hand, my back. Your
fingers, my skin.

*

The distinctly theatrical
slowing of time

close to the hour
of your arrival,

minutes heightened

the way in summer
light after rain sharpens
the fields, the flowers, the grass.

Hones our awareness
for just a few moments that soon
all this, too, will be gone.

*

Buried sides of myself
unearthed like diamonds. You're a ladder

to wideness.

*

Of course I'm walking late
at night, am highly susceptible
to the moon,

the way each of its phases
reminds us of what it was,

what it might be again.

Insular
as a pearl at its fullest.

You see? I can speak now
of nothing but loss.

*

Mostly you're not here
and you're everywhere – a knot

impossible to untie. I learn how
to give up, become

the binding.

*

Alchemical, the heart's juice.

In the coffee shop, the basket
of puckered fruit on the counter

is Caravaggio's bowl, ripe
with saying:
                    beside you,

I can hear everything.

MAKERS

Every minute after midnight
is standing before us:

unfastened gates.

Moonlight painting
one side of your body.

From the streets below,
sounds from the neighbourhood drift
through the open window, unasked

dissolve in shadows
the hour has sown
in the field of this room.

Even the sudden crescendo
of glass created by someone
baptizing a corner

cannot shatter
the stillness here,

the rhythm
we've constructed

from breath.

DISTANCE

Now it is evening. The sun's being
forced to give up its hold on the land,

reluctantly backing its way
out the door.

In the bluing light, a man sits
on a wooden porch, staring across
rutted fields,

watching the tattered line
of the horizon being smudged into charcoal,
wondering if she'll return.

When he thinks of her, she becomes the clouds
streaming across the sky without shoes, smoke
from his cigarette drifting away,

everything he can't hold
in his hands.

For months, her silence was a stranger
at their breakfast table, an old
love that wouldn't be torn from her side.

He'd imagined their lives
as rows in a garden. All this time,
he'd thought
they were planting.

He guesses it's roughly
twelve steps to the car; there's a number
of streets he could travel to find her.

Without thinking,

he begins counting stars as they multiply
above the dark and measured fields

according to the night's equation,

so luminous
and pointed, so far.

UNRESOLVED

The day's retreating back into itself,
leaving its unresolved questions to settle
in the elbows of branches,

cling to the remaining leaves. Dusk gathers
in the corners of this house and stares
at us like a solemn child.

All evening, we'll glide past each other,
enigmatic as late autumn air
shunting the kitchen windows

just to get our attention, then
give no answer.

                    Whatever impression
the hours have made, what
they've left in the diary of their passing
will remain unread. This day's

another sheet of paper being
added to a pile that secretly grows
in the locked drawers of a wooden desk in a room
we stopped entering ages ago.

Tonight, we'll loosen sleeves,
bathe our hands with plates and spoons,
draw the blinds against the moon
compulsively telling its story

and gaze
at the uncreviced face of the clock
until it sends our bodies to bed

where the years will return
in dreams,

come raining back
like the tangled rows
of things that were planted long before

on mornings
when the world was new.

THE PATH BEHIND THE HOUSE

The solemn trees relinquish themselves,
steadily give up the leaves they've housed

and the afternoon disappears
without warning, abandons the only room

it has to provide a bed for the night's
gestation. Even though it's October,

we don't know how to surrender.
This evening, one of us will be walking

the unlit path behind the house, waiting
for the remnants of anger

to fall like an unwanted coat from a shoulder.
Suddenly, someone will notice the moon

in one of its phases – steps
in a dance it's been learning so long –

as it's lifting from the branches so that
it can be seen in its fullness, so that, at last,

it can be held.

JOYRIDE

teenage girl to boy, community addictions centre

I need you like the window needs
the stone in order to speak. You swore
you'd break me of being good.
I'm sick of reflecting the nurse's paid smile,
of showing the social worker my teeth.
In the afternoons, she paws
through my life as if parting the curtains
makes everything clear. I tuck away tears at the session's end
so she can leave
for her house in the country. No streaks I can see.
You give me
a new way to be in the world: how I wanted
to take your wrist in my palm, feel its wild
robin rebellion. To not squeeze,
and call that love.
When you look up
from my body's centre, there's nothing
that needs to be figured out.
Your face is open, matter of fact.
Later, we grin at each other like thieves, slipping
the cuffs
of things that were done to us. What we did back.
Tonight, the stars are all we can see
of the past. Those tiny chips of rearview mirror
remind us the universe runs on collision.
We don't need to be told

these hours are stolen. We're joyriding.
Love's someone else's car.
Tomorrow, I'll be a file again:
they'll open
and close me like drawers in a desk and you'll be back
at the boarding house stepping over
a body asleep in the hall. Those cloudy features adrift
in his bottle not yours. Not yet.
At this moment, your heart's
idling under my ear and the sky's cracked open, big as
a highway. There are no signs
and nowhere to get to but here.

TOOLS

With nothing now,
you've entered this place. Occupancy
an admission of failure: the perceptible

ache of the wooden threshold, sorrow
of the sagging bed.

This motel room north of the city
is a mirror with its face
turned down.

Released from the daily spell of obligations,
you abandon your body
to sleep's waiting sleeve, oblivion

a perfect tool to undo
the seams of your previous life.

                       Unmeasured,
time returns to itself, emerges as being
more liquid than jar and you start to believe
you can live in this way:

at night, car lights travelling
over your sheets in rote
benediction.

Through the walls, the muted chant
of a radio voice floating
towards you.

                          Then one evening,
as the sky's
burrowing further into plum,

a glittery scarf of laughter winds through the air:

some teenagers making their way
through woods, and your mind

instinctively throws out its hand,
grabs hold,

and traipses behind
clear to the creek's edge,

jubilant, tied.

SPRING

arrives like an overdue
love letter.

Like the fair-weather boyfriend
who pulls up one morning out of the blue
in his half-ton, grinning

and you are wilted, dish-water pale
from having been up with the eldest
all night. In spite of yourself,

                    you open your arms.

Spring knows how to get around you.

It knocks at your door, sure of itself, presents
jammed in its pockets:

strands of mauve crocuses,

a handful of robin eggs beaded
with freckles, grass that's picked
its way through snow.

Gifts so close to what you want
you abandon your memory
of other seasons – how you braved

the cellar of winter alone.
The distant stars and cryptic trees
when no one breathed inside your ear.

Those months are history,
diversions, affairs. For weeks
you walk through your bedroom

humming.

COUPLE INDOORS

Inside the cabin,
they're branching together
like lovers from some ancient myth

being braided by fate
into a flower.

Out back, the wind bends
hawkweed into the barren
lap of the ground,

assails lilacs and wild roses.

All evening long, the storm
insists, making its point
like a star debater.

Around midnight,
when it's still advancing
its pragmatic version of things,

the couple answer, planting
kisses along each other's sides
as if they were turning the lights on

one by one
in all the rooms
of a darkened house,

their innocent belief
in the body sturdy as the glass
the rain introduces itself to

just as many times as it
likes before dawn.

BEDS

Plage de l'Aboiteau, Cap-Pelé, New Brunswick

The tapering arc
of a blade of cordgrass

lolling in wind
off the water:

a green hammock for the eye,
its swaying sustains me
all day.

*

Between the white plastic-sided
cottage and the bald

emptiness of the beach,

Acadian dykeland: salty
reed fields of copper, vermillion,
mustard and green.

Colours so profuse, they seem
close to parody. A half-

dozen paint cans kicked
over at once.

*

Woven through the wooden boardwalk's
lattice, berries glinting. Lushly
furtive.

Shades of red –
inscrutable, deep – that speak
of continuance,

augur time.

*

After sleep, how your body
steers towards me

as soon as you come down
the stairs. An unconscious habit
that after a week in this cottage

has turned into ritual.

          In the same way
we look for the nearest window
on waking, to moor

the still half-
dreaming mind,

you find me first. Then
the day.

*

Outside at noon,

looking straight up into
a doorless hall

of bright, pointillated blue

we think maybe somebody
should tell Seurat

his sky's escaped –

the top field of the painting
without dots, gaping

and white.

*

In the backyard, mushrooms
outrageously phallic. Comic-

book funny.

The grass neon, greener
than green.

*

Generous as an unscripted smile,
open arms, the broad sweep of sand dunes
dividing the lip of the beach

from the marram thatch.

Our gaze keeps straying
back to them, pulled from the gravitas
of the ocean's blue pulse

yards from our feet.

                         At nightfall,
walking to the cottage
in the starless air,

we drift
beside this trail of earth-waves
arcing away

from the hard sand beds
that made them.

IV

DIMENSIONS OF RED

Tonight, you and I both know
that in one of the boarding houses downtown,
a young man is waiting

alone in his room for maybe the sixth
or seventh day for an angel to place
a cool hand on his shoulder,

whisper what to do in his ear.

He could die waiting there,
a perfect servant. The evening sky
would continue to gather, rain

fall against the unwashed window,
and the long light that sometimes follows storms
would remind the earth about the vitality

in cycles. In the ditches,
roadside tansy would start to gleam
like thrown coins, meagre lawns
appear succulent and wild roses

smoulder on branches,

knowing nothing but different
dimensions of red.

Even the foil
inside cigarette packages
lining the streets would shine

like the vision of itself

this city will lose in just
a few moments,

the promise made
by the vagrant light that
nothing here

escapes redemption.

RAIN

Surely, this day has been bad
for so many. A leaking cup

of soured plans, botched embraces,
the hand's awkward attempts
at clasping.

Still, the sky's decided to open, let
the rain soak wooden porches, baptize
every paint-chipped rung

while inside a kitchen,
the bad day continues, has limped
into the evening undaunted,

a mouth that's gone
empty too long.

As the rain sweetens the dense
August air that blows in, lifting the hems
of curtains, sighing against beaded screens,

a distraught young father will haul
back his arm. Fold fingers
that have scrubbed potatoes

and buttered bread, his fist
a white impermeable stone.

       Later, his son will sit
in a bedroom, knees drawn
up to meet his chin

as if the separate parts of his body
were mourners leaning against
each other, touch

the only thing that's left
in the long, incomprehensible night.

       Through a window
open in the hall, the bright, metallic
sound of water drenching the earth

will continue for hours

as if to convince him
there is abundance,

as if to heal
the dryness here.

CAREFUL

Now the day's untying itself,

everything that's happened
so far contained in flames of mauves and orange
simmering on the skyline,

fading with the acquiescence
of petals.

      We're tired, and watch
with nothing left to say as evening
enters the land's consciousness: shadows

randomly dousing the sand. Clouds
thinning to a handful of ribbons.

Soon, the beginning stars
will appear: isolate letters
forming on a page we can't see,

and we'll rise from the ground
in silent agreement, start to collect
the things we've carried here

moving careful as deer

because of what's happened
between us,

too cautious

to label it burden
or gift.

MORNING GHAZAL

Your arms fit like a favourite blouse;
an audible click when I put you on.

Brine running from mouth to mouth:
salt, swell. Every single cliché.

It's midnight. We're still talking. The world
at the kitchen table, pulsating. Near.

Fingers laced, we're a TV couple,
blended ingredients in a cake.

In the early orange copper of morning,
we pull apart like bees from flowers. Faces soaked.

WHEN THE HEART BELIEVES IT'S
FOUND A HOME

Neighbourhoods evaporate. Street signs blur.
In the hardest parts of town, an Impressionist painting
marks every corner. The heart navigates
like a local, coat unbuttoned, common sense

lagging like a mother's cries. It slows, passing
a pawnshop window, noticing the hairline crack winding
through a chipped teacup's blue lilies. The heart
frantically searches pockets lined only with pennies and lint.

At noon, you see it sprawled on a bench
near the intersection, calmly blowing perfect smoke rings,
forehead tipped to an undisturbed carpet of sky,
that room without corners. Late in the day, the heart

takes the same route through the city,
greets every squeegee kid by name, and winds up
in a rundown hotel where it walks the length of corridors
strewn with boot marks and burns,

stops before a presswood door. Once inside, it pulls
from its jacket a feather duster, a bucket and broom.
Later, as the sun's sinking into the velvet plush
of the horizon, the heart stares past the untouched plates,

studying the gathering dark. Night
has custody of the children, has lured them
to a downtown corner where they'll solemnly
follow desires as if each one were the path to a garden.

The heart wipes the mouths of empty glasses,
makes a list for tomorrow's meal, lets itself out
and retraces steps through neon streets.
At daybreak,

it stands watching the gulls spiralling
high above the harbour, waiting for the morning's gold
so that it can return to the same old staircase, fingers
clutching a single key. Bound

to an impulse fierce as the sea
knocking against a resolute shore: to unlock
door after door after door.

PARTICULARS

How're the beet greens?

Third time in an hour. He's drunk,
hanging onto particulars like they
were banister rails.

This morning, he sent a basket of vegetables
over with his son come to play with
my daughter. Ushered me in

when I brought his boy home, sorting
through air for something between us
that might take root.

How're the beet greens?

As if they were roses.

He nods reflexively as I thank him,
shuffles a kettle onto a burner and perches
at the edge of a kitchen chair. Without
looking up, he reaches back, lifts a guitar

from the floor behind him and starts
tracking the wandering chords of a song
I haven't heard in years.

Something spirited in the voice
still knows how to run.

He shakes my praise like a dog
sprays water. *Take Willie, now, Willie ...*
he demurs, handing the song
to its original owner.

In the living room, records are stacked
in piles oracular as standing stones.

He tells me he had even more
until his father came home one night
from the bar, sat down on the couch

and rhythmically broke every one
he could reach across his knee.

Says he can still see the look of surprise
on the garbage man's face as he tried
the next morning to lift the bag

from the curb, was carried
back to earth by the weight.

He grins at this, lines winging out
from eyes that have beat for thirty-eight years
against the world's delivery room light.

Then he straightens up suddenly,
called by something.

What's the matter with him?

My daughter, rounding the corner
for her jacket, sees him staring,
arrested by walls.

Ssshh.

I swear there's something
in him trying to rise.

STILL LIFE

Sunflowers, 1888, National Gallery

I can't stare at that painting; there's no place to rest. The
eye, sleepless vagrant, cannot make its bed in a building
frantically being cleared. All those flowers stampeding,
storming the painting like they're running from a house on
fire. Rapunzels leaning out of their tower, wide-eyed,
scanning the ground below knowing they'll have to leap.

Once, the good earth was under their feet. The sky above,
unceilinged cathedral. Then, one day, the Stranger waist-
deep in their midst. Dragging behind him that rickety altar.
His mirror. All day, his face twisting towards it.

Slicing through the morning score of birds, grass, leaves –
the hammer of brushstrokes knocking: clotted fists donning
different coloured gloves, trying to match the fabric of day.
Meanwhile, the sunflowers sway to the music, ladies with
fans, each breeze a brand new partner to waltz with.
Watching, the Stranger turns with his easel, awkwardly tries
to follow their steps. Suddenly forces his way to the floor.
Wants to cut in.

In the studio now. The yellow house. The sunflowers shown
a room in the vase: transients nibbling sweets in the parlour,
pulling absently at their ties. Choked. Like Vincent all his
life, collared by Goupil's, the gospels, the mines. Later, the
iron fist of his fits.

Panicked, the visitors pace the floor when they see there's no key on the table. Understanding pushes its way through their petals, twists their furious stems. Every inch single-minded, groping for light.

Sighing, Vincent opens the door, paints them streaming out of their cell – a classroom of kids running outside for recess, amber wine spilling out of its skin. Butterflies bursting from their apartments, suitcases packed.

From the blue cocoon of his broken heart, Vincent starts another letter. Pledges in paint to remember them always. Captures his love. Their gorgeous good-bye.

CROSSING THE FIELD

The day's an old room
stripped of its furniture; there are
never enough beds in winter.

By late afternoon, the shadows
are forming a blue inconsolable hall

as sparrows retreat to makeshift
cots of pine bark and eaves.

Even the parched marsh grass
has stilled, every blade
become an ear.

Crossing the field in this
changing air as the landscape
rearranges itself,

we can feel the weight
of night on our foreheads,

sense the coming

of unravelled thought
and missing light,

hear something calling us
home by name.

MILL ROAD

And then, you begin imagining
grace as something that isn't bestowed
or attained, but perceived,

residing.

Months after the accident, you're standing
at the railway crossing by the old
woollen mill, watching wind-

clawed stalks of goldenrod
bow with the force of a passing train.

Not far away, in a basement
flat, a tired woman
is helping an anxious child with homework.

In his stammering hand, the pencil
meets, then withdraws from the page
like a finger yanked

from fire. In hot frustration, he raises
his head, sees the way his mother's smile
smoothes the contours of her face,

and thinks of afternoon light
striking his things on the dresser.

How it makes them
even more like themselves.

In the parking lot
behind their building, a man wrapped

in the caul of an army
blanket is sleeping against a billboard's
metal spine.

In the cavern
made by the inch between the fabric
and his parted mouth,

his breath's warming,
anointing his skin while, around him,
the evening condenses,

distills itself into the darkness

that will soften the corners of street signs
and doors, erase the division
between rooftops

and the unmeasured sky.

ACKNOWLEDGMENTS

Earlier versions of some of these poems have appeared in the following publications: *The Antigonish Review, Dandelion, The Fiddlehead, Kaleidoscope, The Literary Review of Canada, The New Quarterly, Prairie Fire, Prism International, Pottersfield Portfolio,* and *Windsor Review.* Poems also appeared in *Poet to Poet: Poems Written to Poets and the Stories that Inspired Them* (Guernica, 2012), *Undercurrents: New Voices in Canadian Poetry* (Cormorant, 2011), *Landmarks: An Anthology of New Atlantic Canadian Poetry of the Land* (Acorn Press, 2001), and *Vintage 2000: League of Canadian Poets Anthology* (Ronsdale Press, 2000).

An earlier version of this manuscript won the Alfred G. Bailey Award from the Writers Federation of New Brunswick. Earlier versions of "Spring," "Weekday Morning Songs," and "When the Heart Believes It's Found a Home" were shortlisted in *Arc*'s Poem of the Year Contest. "Spring" was shortlisted in the *Prism International* Poetry Contest. "The Path Behind the House," "Broken," and "Dimensions of Red" were nominated for a National Magazine Award. An earlier version of "Rain" was selected as one of the "Notable Poems of 2015" listed in the *Best Canadian Poetry in English 2015.* My sincere thanks to all of the editors involved.

I am grateful to the Canada Council for the Arts and the Nova Scotia Department of Tourism, Culture and Heritage for the financial assistance that enabled me to write these poems.

6936

My sincere thanks to Allan Hepburn for his editorial suggestions and warm support, and to Ryan Van Huijstee, Mark Abley, and Carolyn Smart for their gracious help and enthusiasm.

My thanks, as well, to Brian Bartlett, Peter Sanger, and Robyn Sarah for their generosity, kindness, and encouragement.

I am deeply grateful to my family, writing colleagues, and friends for their patience, love, and support during the writing of these poems.

*

"Fireflies" is for Jan Zwicky. "Seeing Me Home" is for David Adams Richards. "Waiting" is for Sandra Barry. "For Paul, Away" is for Paul Émile d'Entremont. "Beds" is for Robert Christian.

*

This book is for Jenn, beautiful daughter.